The
WINNING EDGE

The Secrets and Techniques
of the World's Best Cricketers

by

Jack Potter
inaugural head coach, Australian Cricket Academy

and

Ashley Mote
author, 'The Glory Days of Cricket'
(The Cricket Society Literary Award, 1997)

WITH A FOREWORD BY SHANE WARNE

The Parrs Wood Press
MANCHESTER

First Published 2001

THE PARRS WOOD PRESS
St Wilfrid's Enterprise Centre
Royce Road, Manchester, M15 5BJ
www.parrswoodpress.com

ISBN: 1 903158 18 4

This book was produced by Andrew Searle and Helen Faulkner of The Parrs Wood Press and Printed in Great Britain by:

Fretwell Print and Design
Healey Works
Goulbourne Street
Keighley
West Yorkshire BD21 1PZ

THE WINNING EDGE

The Secrets and Techniques of the World's Best Cricketers

**improve your game
analyse your performances
overcome your weaknesses
understand your strengths
build your confidence**

WIN AT CRICKET

CONTENTS

Enclosure: CD-rom

FOREWORD

by Shane Warne

I HAVE GREAT PLEASURE in supporting Jack Potter's book. It looks at cricket coaching from a different and extremely important perspective. I am certain it will help players at every level to improve their game.

The Winning Edge comes from a fine source. During the 1980's, Australian cricket was struggling. We had been beaten by New Zealand, England and the West Indies. In 1986, with the support of the Prime Minister, Bob Hawke, the Australian Cricket Board and the Australian Institute of Sport decided drastic action was needed. Together, they took a gamble and started The Australian Cricket Academy. The following year, after a world-wide search, Jack Potter was appointed the inaugural Head Coach, and I was lucky enough to be chosen as one of his earliest students.

Life was tough for both staff and students in those early days. Jack arrived in Adelaide in 1987 with no facilities, no program, one assistant and plenty of doubters. The Australian Cricket Board gave him a free rein and an awesome brief - make Australian cricket the best! State cricket organisations were asked to nominate their most promising young players for a year-long program of personal development. But most of the states didn't want to lose these potential future stars to Adelaide. They claimed that the players would get stale, bored, and lose interest. There were even suggestions that the quality of the coaching would be no better than in their own states.

So, a difficult beginning for a program that has since proved to be the world's benchmark in cricket coaching and preparation, and the envy of all cricket-playing nations. The Academy provided the spark which took Australia to the top of the cricketing world in less than a decade, and it's no surprise that most cricketing countries have since set up their own Academies based on the model established in Adelaide in 1988.

At that time, Jack Potter's ideas and development programs were truly revolutionary. He knew that if Australia was to become the world's top cricketing nation, the players had to work harder than anyone else, and then some. So, while other countries sat back and watched, the Cricket Academy turned Australia's young hopefuls into athletes, through innovative programs of weight-training, fitness work, diet, psychological preparation, injury prevention, record keeping, target and achievement setting and - last but not least - technique training.

By the end of each demanding but unforgettable year the students had become stronger, faster, physically flexible, more technically proficient, mentally tougher, and - eventually - totally confident in themselves both as players and as a team.

At one stage in the 90's most of the Australian Test or One Day Team consisted of graduates of the Cricket Academy - including Michael Slater, Justin Langer, Michael Bevan, Brendon Julian, Adam Gilchrist, Greg Blewett, Stuart Law, Damien Martyn and yours truly Shane Warne. Even England has benefited from the Australian Academy by selecting players like Craig White, Martin McCague and Jason Gallian.

Today, almost all state players in Australia, and current Test players, have spent time at the Cricket Academy and benefited from its innovative training and techniques.

So it is not surprising to me that Jack, and his co-author Ashley Mote, have come up with a coaching book that is stimulating, thought-provoking and different. Now, at last, every player - whatever their present standard - can share in, and use, the personal development techniques which took some of us all the way to the top of this wonderful game.

But this is not a book that teaches anything about the techniques of batting, bowling, fielding or wicket-keeping. It is a book that helps improve performance. It explains how to use your brains, set goals, keep records and gain confidence.

Young players who read this book, and use the accompanying CD-rom, can be guaranteed to improve their cricket. They will learn to think positively, aggressively and fast. They will know how to organise themselves and play their full part in their team. Above all, they will know the value of commitment, and how to deliver it on the cricket field.

That is what Jack taught us. Now, through this book, everyone can benefit from the same ideas.

You can see that Jack Potter had a great influence on the vital formative part of my career. So, for that reason and many others, I warmly recommend The Winning Edge to players, coaches and students of cricket alike. I hope they will use it wisely and well.

INTRODUCTION

This slim volume is all about improving your performance on the cricket field. It doesn't matter what standard of cricket you play, or want to play. Nor does it matter whether you bat, bowl, keep wicket or are picked for your fielding alone.

Here, you will not find...how to play this or that shot...bowl this or that delivery...catch the ball...or field and return it to the wicket-keeper. There are many other coaching manuals that give you that practical "how to" advice.

Yet these few pages pack a powerful punch. They reveal the secrets and techniques used by some of the best players in the world. Those great sportsmen used these ideas to reach the top, and they used them to stay there. Now - you can use them too.

The ideas and methods revealed in this book will improve your cricket and your enjoyment of the game. They will also help you to become an even more valuable member of your team.

The CD With This Book

With this book comes a CD for your computer. On it are shots of three famous modern test players when they were unknown students - Shane Warne and Justin Langer (Australia), and Craig White (England). All three were coached as young men by Jack Potter. You will also see both authors talking about the importance of the mental approach to cricket.

But to get the most out of the CD you need to read this book first. Then you'll know how best to use all the charts we've included. They are set up on the CD so that you can copy them many times over. Then, you just complete one each time it is appropriate.

That facility makes this the first inter-active cricket coaching manual ever published. It gives you the tools to develop your game, and the means to check your success.

Use these personal records and practice schedules regularly. You can also store all the results on your computer. File them in date order so that you can see the progress you're making over the seasons.

That way you'll not only improve your game, but you can enjoy watching your own achievements.

And you'll have even more fun from this greatest of all games - cricket.

Good luck!

1.

REACHING YOUR FULL POTENTIAL

Why do some players succeed and others fail to reach their full potential? Many have similar physical skills, and are much the same in fitness and other characteristics. Often, it's no more than a few small - but crucial - differences between individuals that determine who goes all the way and who doesn't.

The following points illustrate the areas you can develop to reach your full potential.

Dedication and Determination

By recognising the importance of these two personal qualities you will develop the desire to succeed, gain confidence and work hard. Your endeavour will improve and training will become more focused. Practising skills, working on your fitness, and achieving mental toughness, will together enable you to achieve your goals.

High Expectations

Players with high expectations will not be satisfied just to be playing low level competitive cricket. They will have their sights set on a higher target – playing at the highest level of cricket. And they will have the required discipline to get there.

Look at the qualities on the chart and mark the areas where you think you are strong. See the gaps? Now you know exactly where you need to work hard to make yourself strong in all areas.

Skill

With correct practice, it is possible to improve your skill level. So practise with a purpose - the purpose to improve. The more purposeful your practice the more your skill will improve. Remember the adage: "Right practice makes progress."

Fitness

Every sportsman should work on fitness. It will improve every facet of your game as well as helping to prevent injury. Hand/eye co-ordination is equally crucial to your success, and there are methods of improving it.

Confidence

Cricket, more than any other game, depends on confidence. The most talented player can lose form because of a lack of confidence. It is very important to develop mental strategies that assist your self-confidence.

Goal Setting

This part of your game is as important as any other, yet it is often not fully appreciated. By setting goals designed to improve your performance you can become a significantly better player.

Patience

Whether you are batting, bowling or fielding, patience is a vital mental quality. Patience assists your concentration. There is everything to be gained by waiting for the right moment to pounce. Control your eagerness, and turn it to your advantage.

Mental Toughness

The best players believe in themselves, whatever the situation. There are times when your courage will be tested. You will be respected by your team-mates and the opposition if you can develop mental toughness and not choke under pressure. This quality will enable you to perform in any situation, when others around you may be found wanting. Try to be the person who can be relied on when the going gets tough. Always be confident of your own ability to cope.

Discipline

To achieve anything in sport you have to be self-disciplined. This means working at your game and practising when you feel like it and also when you don't. It is sometimes difficult to do this, but by having achievable goals, and remaining focused, you will improve both your game and your performances.

Nous

This can best be described as being "cricket smart" – a sort of sixth sense about a situation and being able to read the game at any given moment. Some players have this sense. An example might be a captain changing the field placings, or making a bowling change, without any apparent reason...but it results in a wicket falling. Batsmen sometimes change their approach against a particular bowler so that they can start to dominate him.

These crucial, sometimes instinctive, decisions are not taught in any coaching manuals. But players can make a valuable contribution to their team and their own game by being prepared to think slightly differently about each challenge that emerges for them during the course of a game. It doesn't matter how an idea gets into your head. If it does, it's probably worth a try.

The ideas which follow in this manual will help you to develop all these vital skills and qualities.

HOW CAN I REACH
MY FULL POTENTIAL?

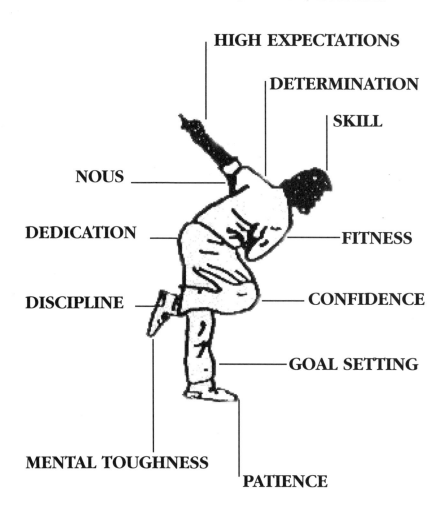

HIGH EXPECTATIONS

DETERMINATION

SKILL

NOUS

DEDICATION

FITNESS

DISCIPLINE

CONFIDENCE

GOAL SETTING

MENTAL TOUGHNESS

PATIENCE

2.

GAME PREPARATION
(Plans and goals)

In any contest, to perform well you must prepare well. Each of us learns to prepare in the way that suits us best. We all have our different methods, which will be determined by many factors. An understanding of your psychological make-up will help you.

Some players are naturally quiet. Some get very nervous before a game. Some are noisy and apparently confident. Others may be a combination of all these characteristics.

Some players like to open the batting because they can't bear to sit around and watch. If they are asked to bat down the order, they get so tensed up that they can't relax when they finally get to the wicket. Others hate opening for exactly the same reasons – they can't relax in that situation. It's too much for them. The circumstances are quite different, but the response is the same.

Whatever your personality, and preferences, it is vital that you have a personal game plan. This is different from the team plan. These are your own personal goals for each game. Your coach should help you choose your goals, and these may vary between games.

If you're in form and doing well, you can raise your goals. If you've been having a hard time lately, your immediate goals may have more to do with restoring your confidence than with making a spectacular individual contribution to the team's effort. In any case, restoring your confidence will probably lead directly to a fine individual performance.

Your goals may also vary with the standard of cricket you are playing. For example, you may be an opening batsman or an opening bowler for your school team. In a slightly higher grade, you may be used as a stock bowler or middle-order batsman. And until you establish yourself in a much higher grade, you may be regarded as a change bowler or lower-order batsman.

Here's an idea to help you perform better. It helps to build confidence, it helps generate enthusiasm and increases your ability to do well.

Each time you play, make the time and effort to write down in detail your targets for today's game. This will give you a structured and positive approach. It will help you to think constructively about each game. It will set goals by which to measure your achievements. And you will gain enormously from the self-discipline involved.

This type of preparation helps to overcome nerves. In any sporting contest, nervousness is caused by uncertainty. If we are not sure about something then it pre-occupies our thoughts. So the setting of specific targets helps eliminate those worries.

And here's some more tips for before a match:

* Find out as much as you can about the opposition.

* How does the wicket usually play?

* Is it easy for players to see the ball around the ground?

* Do their main bowlers have any specially deceiving deliveries?

* What sort of tactics are they likely to use?

Little details like these build up a picture of the contest to come, and help you to plan for it. It's all common sense, really, but using these routines will help to give you the winning edge.

Short-term goals

Here are a few examples of short-term goals which you can use to build your expectations and performance.

Batsmen:

As an opener, my first and most important goal is to stay in for at least half an hour, and help take the shine off the new ball. (Not only is this the main job of an opener, but it also enables the rest of the team to see how the wicket is playing and what the bowlers are doing.)

Once I have blunted their fast attack, I can then start to build my innings and score more freely.

Today I am going to leave rising balls outside my off-stump. Today I am going to bat in 10's.

I am going to hook and cut only after I have scored 30.

Today I am going to bat for at least two hours.

I will watch my running between the wickets.

I will put a very large value on my wicket.

I will keep balanced, and still. I will move only when the ball is bowled. If I am balanced, I can go back or forward with equal ease.

I will move my feet to get side-on to where I want the ball to go.

I will keep my head level, and still. Whatever else I move, my head stays still.

I will watch the bowler's face during the run-up, and his hand as he bowls. I will ignore the rest of his body! I will try to pick up the spin or seam quickly, and follow the ball right onto the bat.

I will relax the grip of my bottom hand. My top hand will do all the work - backlift, power through the line of the ball, and follow-through in the direction the ball is hit.

If I face a short delivery, I will get my hands at least as high as the ball.

Bowlers:

My first and most important goal is to get my line and length right.

I will try to bowl every ball down the "corridor of uncertainty".

I will concentrate on getting my action right, so that my rhythm is good.

I will think the batsman out.

When I have bowled five dot balls, I will put more pressure on the batsman by bowling a maiden.

I will remain positive, regardless of the batsman.

I will bowl at the imaginary target, just on a length, which I have been practising so successfully.

If the batsman moves his feet before I bowl, I will deliver the ball he's not expecting - full length if he's gone back, short if he's come forward.

If he constantly edges forward as I bowl, I will keep the ball just short of a length on middle and leg.

If the batsman grips his bat tightly with his lower hand, I will bowl well up to him. He'll have difficulty playing the ball with a straight bat.

Fielders:

I will support my bowlers today with good fielding and encouragement.

I will try to run out three people today.

I will be totally confident and positive, enthusiastic and alert.

I hope someone hits a catch to me.

I will save 30 runs in the field.

I will concentrate on my throwing action, which I have been practising so successfully.

My ground fielding and throwing will be brilliant.

I will back up every throw, and encourage others to do the same.

Wicket-Keepers:

I will not let any byes through.

I will concentrate on every ball as if a catch is coming.

I will stay low when taking the spinners.

I will catch everything that comes my way.

I will be very neat in everything I do, and so inspire the rest of the team.

I will encourage good fielding.

Everyone:

When I'm on the field, I will focus on every delivery as if my life depended on it.

No matter what, I will do well.

On the next page is a simple framework for your preparation for each game. Using this chart will help improve your performances. Fill one in before each match.

Use the charts to trigger questions about your performance and those aspects of the game on which you need to work even harder.

For example, ask yourself – if something in your game is not going as well as it should – what new methods of practice to adopt. Do you need to change tactics during a game, or even in the nets? Do you need more practice on certain types of wickets or ground conditions, or against particular sorts of bowlers or batsmen? If a pattern emerges, try to learn from it, and discuss how to deal with it with your coach. If he makes a suggestion, or offers a solution, never forget he can't make the improvement for you. Only you can do that.

After every game, make notes of your actual achievements against your goals, and keep the charts so that you can enjoy watching your progress over the seasons.

The Winning Edge

My Goals for This Game

Match_____v_____

Played at_____Date_____

MY MOST IMPORTANT GOAL _____
_____-_____

My other goals:

1._____
2._____
3._____
4._____

Game Preparation

Likely Conditions_____
Opposition's strengths_____
Opposition's weaknesses_____

Strategies to achieve goals – in the nets

1_____
2_____
3_____

Strategies to achieve goals – on the day and in my head

1. *Determination*
2. *Concentrate and relax*
3. *Focus*
4. *Never give up – come what may*
5_____
6_____

Plan A to achieve goals – on the day and on the field

1_____
2_____
3_____

Plan B on the day, if plan A isn't working_____

Game Review (Performance rating 1-10)

Batting_____
Bowling_____
Fielding_____
Wicket-keeping_____
Tactics_____
Concentration_____
Handling pressure_____
Calmness and control_____
Overcomjng setbacks_____
TOTAL TODAY_____

Comments and notes for action before the next match_____

This chart can be printed out from the CD-rom

19

Setting Personal Goals

One of the most extraordinary documents ever written by a first-class player must be the "personal budget" prepared by Richard Hadlee at the beginning of his 1984 season as the overseas player at Nottinghamshire. He kept it with him throughout the season. It read:

Goals:

1. First to 100 wickets
2. Better career best bowling of 7-23
3. Ten bags of five wickets
4. Sixty wickets at home, forty away
5. Better career-best batting
6. 600 runs away, 400 at home
7. Three centuries and six fifties
8. The double (100 wickets, 1000 runs)
9. Player of the year
10. All-rounder of the year
11. I must help win 10 matches in the championship with an inspired individual performance
12. Take 25 catches

He budgeted 20 championship matches, but played in 24
He budgeted 31 innings and played 33
He targeted 1000 runs and got 1179
He targeted a batting average of 34. It was 51.2
He estimated bowling 750 overs, and bowled 772
He budgeted 250 maidens, and bowled 248
He expected to give away 1500 runs and gave away 1645
His 100 wicket target turned out to be 117
He targeted a bowling average of 15. It was 14.05

This is what makes great players.

But how many players do you know - at any level - who prepare such a document at the beginning of each season? How many have ever thought about producing one?

Using Richard Hadlee's goals as a model, try setting your own specific goals for next season - or the rest of this one. Be realistic, think about each department of the game, and settle on targets that you can achieve - but only if you regularly perform exceptionally well.

And when the going gets tough, if you fall behind - don't change the targets. Instead, re-double your efforts.

That's what the great players do.
Now, you can do the same.

3.

OVERCOMING ANXIETY

It has been suggested that 70 per cent of a cricketer's success is determined by what goes on in his head. So learning to deal with anxiety, and replacing it with some degree of mental toughness, is crucial.

At some stage in their career, almost every cricketer has felt nervous about their next game. The more important the occasion, the more the butterflies appear. Even at the highest level – test cricket – where the cricketers are exceptionally talented and very experienced, many individuals suffer attacks of nerves.

There is nothing new, or wrong, in this. And it only becomes a problem if the sufferer allows the attack to affect his performance. And that applies to us all. So, when do players get nervous?

Here are some of the most common situations:

Batsmen:

The night before an important game.
The morning of a game.
Before the toss.
Waiting to bat.
Walking onto the ground.
Before they've scored.
Until they've reached double figures.
When the wicket is difficult – even in the nets.

Bowlers:

The night before an important game.
The morning of the game.
Before the toss.
Before their first over.
In a tight situation.
Bowling to a very good batsman.
When line and length go awry.
When their rhythm isn't right.

Interesting, isn't it, that both batsmen and bowlers suffer nervousness from the same causes. So, if you're nervous, never forget that the man at the other end may be feeling even worse than you are! Control your nerves first and you may turn the match in your favour.

The best way is to use a few simple and positive thoughts.

Dealing with Anxiety

There are several ways to overcome these pre-match nerves. Most are quite simple and easy to use.

1. Replace negative thoughts with positive ones

If the opposition has a good away-swing bowler, stop thinking about how good he is. Instead, say to yourself: "That doesn't worry me. I've been batting against away-swing bowling for ever. I've practised in the nets against it this week. I can handle him. In fact, he may have a problem with me."

This technique can be applied to any competitive situation. So whenever a negative thought occurs, use a trigger mechanism - slap your thigh, for instance - and replace the negative thought with a positive one. Think about the problems you can set for him. Think about how nervous he is. Think about how you can add to his nervousness.

2. See yourself performing well

Many top sportsmen use this technique. But it takes a little practice: Find a quiet corner, shut your eyes, and as vividly as possible, try to "see" yourself playing a particular shot - bowling a particular ball - whatever you want to do. Concentrate hard - "see" the details, the surroundings, the colours even. Play the "film" over and over in your mind. Gradually, with practice, these scenes will become so real that they will transfer themselves into your life on the field! This is the power of positive thinking.

3. Believe in yourself - and the confidence will follow

Each game is an opportunity - an experience to enjoy, an opportunity to shine in the eyes of your team, to show them how good you are. Simply forget the pressures. Make a conscious decision that you are going to enjoy your cricket, whatever the outcome. And then just do it.

4. Focus yourself

Control your breathing and you control your nerves. Again, it takes a little practice. Here's how...

Inhale a deep, slow, breath. Take four or five seconds. Count them. Then try to feel your diaphragm sink into your stomach and down towards your groin. Hold for two seconds. Then - just as slowly - exhale, releasing the air in a controlled way from the bottom up.

You have focused attention on your body, and you have controlled it. You have also focused your concentration. Now relax the body, but keep the concentration - on the game.

5. Use your ritual

Almost all players have rituals - the way they change for a match, put their pads on, stay quiet, make a lot of noise, whatever. We each have a way of getting ready. Use these routines positively. They do help prepare you for a game. There's no need to invent more. But don't be shy of the ones you have already. Use them as a source of comfort and reassurance as you focus your thoughts and concentrate on what you want to achieve today.

6. Anticipate each segment of the game

Every part of the game is a segment of the whole. Even getting ready to bat, or marking out your run - both are segments. At each stage of the game, get to know what comes next for you. Think about what you are going to do before it happens.

If you are opening the innings, for instance, think specifically about the techniques needed to do well - defend or let the good balls go, especially at the start; play only the shots you are good at; don't fend at balls outside off stump; eliminate the shots that get you out.

At every stage of a game, each player should be anticipating what is required of him in the next few minutes. Get used to applying this way of thinking.

7. Relaxation and concentration

You are playing in today's game because someone thought you were good enough. You have enough talent and skill to be here.

So - whatever you're doing - batting, bowling, fielding - try to focus just on what you're doing right now. Don't worry about who might win at the end.

And don't think about the mechanics of what you're doing. It's a strange thing, but if you let your body play instinctively, it will do better than if you consciously tell it what to do.

Cricket is played one ball at a time. The last ball is gone, whatever happened. The next one is the only one that matters. Just concentrate on that one.

Batsmen - focus totally on the ball being bowled, and let your instincts determine your response. Cut yourself off from the surroundings. Connect mentally with the ball. Concentrate on it to the exclusion of all else. With a quiet, focused mind you can trust your instincts, be at one with the game, relax and let go. Enjoy the shot - almost watch yourself playing it.

Between deliveries, look at the gaps in the field, not at the fielders. Gradually build up a memory of the gaps.

Building a big innings is no more than taking many small steps. Here are the first few reminders from the start:

...First, I am not going to let them have my wicket.
...Carefully to 10. No risks, safe shots only.
...Almost as carefully to 20. Still no risks.

...Now another 10.

...And another.

...What's the total - ok, lets get another 25 before we

...lose another wicket.

...Now another 25.

...And another.

...And so on...

...I will never give my wicket away, however many I've scored.

...Today, I'm going to be "not out" at the end.

Bowlers - decide what your next delivery will be, and then focus totally on the scene at the other end. Not the batsman, necessarily, but the spot where you want the ball to land. Keep your mind on that, and let your body do the work naturally.

Fielders - focus on the batsman to the exclusion of all else. Follow the stroke, and react even quicker than he does.

Wicket-keepers - watch the ball all the way down.

Everyone - commit yourself to awareness, not to conscious effort.

Don't think. Simply be aware, as sharply aware as possible - and allow your body to respond instinctively!

8. Ask yourself - what's the worst that can happen?

Tomorrow the game is over, and mostly forgotten. Meanwhile, the worst that could happen is:

* You could get injured - not very likely.
* You could get a duck - possible, but so what?
* You could make a low score, or not take any wickets - better luck next time.
* You let the team, yourself, your family, down - but they won't love you any the less.

With the preparation we have outlined, you could even succeed.

Now there's a thought!

4.

DETERMINATION TO SUCCEED

There are two routes to success in almost any walk of life, including sport. Natural ability – and determination.

Curiously enough, few people have both in equal measure. One of these two qualities usually dominates the progress and performance of each individual.

Gifted batsmen like Brian Lara, Sachin Tendulkar and the Waugh twins have extraordinary natural talent. They make the game look ridiculously easy. They seem to have so much time to play their shots, which are then timed and placed to perfection. Few players are born so lucky.

We admire them, but we cannot hope to emulate them. Nor should we try.

For most of us, natural ability is no more than average. We practise and improve our skills. But we have to rely on our determination if we are to be truly successful. Even as gifted a player as Tendulkar says that "hunger" is the difference between a good player and a great one. "It's the will to perform well that makes the difference." That's a statement which is true at every level of the game.

Some of the greatest cricketers of all time used determination to build on whatever natural talent they had. Even WG Grace and Don Bradman fall into this category. Of course, they had great talent, but what was exceptional was their determination, and that was something they developed for themselves.

Whatever standard of cricket you play, you can do the same. You can use determination to go much further than your talent might take you on its own.

Ask yourself – would I rather have eleven determined players in my team, or eleven gifted ones? Which is the team that'll try hard only when it suits them? Which is the team that's going to battle to the very end when you're in trouble? Which is the team most likely to win?

Look around the team you play for now. Which three batsmen and bowlers would you want to bat or bowl for you if your very life depended on it? Now ask yourself why you selected those individuals. And whether you might have been on their list of three.

Make up your mind to be a certain selection in future.

Determination is not difficult to develop. It's an attitude, a way of thinking, an accumulation of many little differences between you and the next man. It's also a very private quality. People don't claim to be determined. They just are. The determined player doesn't boast about it, perhaps doesn't even want others to notice, although they probably will.

He's not working harder to impress anybody. He's working harder simply because he wants to be successful as a player and as valuable a member of the team as possible.

The determined player is the one who runs a few extra laps after training, increases his speed training, uses the weight training room for longer, and who practises fielding and throwing, batting and bowling in the nets when everyone else has finished or wants to finish.

Success may not come more easily, either. Determined players often have to struggle to do the things that other, more talented players do with apparent ease. They catch up by working harder, by being more determined to succeed.

Use this simple list to develop your own determination:

Be the first to training sessions and the nets, and the last to leave.

Use your time to practise. Don't stand around talking to others. Make sure you achieve more during each session than anyone else.

Set aside some time to attempt something a little beyond you, or something neither you nor anyone else in the team can do well. For example, try slip catching with one hand only, or get bouncers bowled at you down the line of the leg stump.

Set high achievement goals for each net practice. Treat it as a match. If you're a batsman, spend plenty of time practising the shots you find difficult. Don't waste time on the shots you find easy. Ask the bowlers who trouble you most to bowl at you most. And ask the best bowlers to bowl at you. Bowlers should apply the same principles in reverse.

Test yourself against the best whenever you can, for as long as you can.

If you're having trouble with an aspect of the game, set tough targets for yourself. For instance, have a net without wearing pads if you want to improve your leg-side play, or practise playing off the back foot without wearing gloves. (The West Indians used these ideas as early as the 1950s.) Practise· playing spin on the roughest surface you can find.

Offer to do the tough jobs in a match. Go the extra yard, give that extra 10 per cent, and your actions will lift the whole side. Offer to go in next when batting is difficult. Offer to bowl the last few overs in a tight situation.

Set goals for yourself all the time. Even during a game, think how you can make a difference right now – and then do it. For example: I must increase the run rate *and* not get out; my next over will be a wicket-maiden.

Be the person the captain and the team can rely on – now and always.

Never give in.

These are the techniques that will enable you to develop your determination, and which will more than make up for any lack of natural ability.

And here is the really good news. Over the years, dozens of cricketers with no more than average natural ability eventually reached the top and played in test matches. Their success proves that hard work can take you all the way.

5.

HAVING A HARD TIME?

Occasionally you'll have a run of poor performances. It happens to us all. But if it goes on too long, it can start to prey on your mind and become a downwards spiral. You need to break out of it quickly. And here's how.

Don't waste time finding excuses – poor umpiring, difficult wicket, whatever. Make up your mind that you're going to change things around, starting now.

Commit yourself to a change of attitude and technique for the next game. Think positively about how you can improve. Try to analyse what you need to do better. What is going wrong? Why? What should you do that you have not been doing? What are your strengths?

Think about the first-class players you admire. Ask yourself, what would they have done in your last match? How would they have played? Replay your previous innings or bowling spell in your own mind, and "see" what you should have done better. Replay the ball that got you out. But this time play it safely.

And when your next game starts, remember that the other side probably doesn't know you've been having a difficult time lately. So be positive and walk to the crease as if you mean business. Look confident and be confident. Your body-language is important to you, and it sends a signal to the other team. Even if you don't feel too confident inside, make sure you give the right aggressive signals to the opposition.

Lift your game. Play like a professional. If your ambition is to play exceptionally well in your present grade of cricket, or you aspire to play in a higher grade of cricket one day, play like it today. Once you played schools cricket. Now its grade, or league, or first-class. Whatever the standard, you're here because someone thought you're good enough.

Today you're going to prove them right. So start as you mean to go on – absolutely determined to succeed. Not tomorrow, not next week, but today.

Today you are going to make a big contribution to a winning team.

Start by relying on your strengths. Just play your best shots and hit them hard, or bowl your stock delivery on line and length. Get the good things going well.

Then, as your confidence returns, that's the moment to raise your standards and personal expectations to exceed those playing against you. Now hit your best shots even harder. Look for chances to score off deliveries you might have previously left alone - the nearly half-volley, the not quite short ball. Or start bowling the unexpected delivery.

In a nutshell, let the other team begin to worry about you.

6.

ANALYSING YOUR GAME

Use this personal analysis regularly to check your progress and to identify the areas you need to work on next.

Personal Analysis

Batting	Present Level	Improvement Needed
	Fair – Good – Excellent	Small - Large

Fast bowling-
letting good ball go
- back foot shots
- front foot shots

Slow bowling
- reading spin
Off spin
- back foot shots
- front foot shots
Leg spin
- back foot shots
- front foot shots

The Winning Edge

Playing swing bowling _____ | _____
Working singles _____ | _____
Playing the short ball _____ | _____
Attacking the short ball _____ | _____
Off-stump judgement _____ | _____
Footwork _____ | _____
Awareness _____ |
Aspects Needing Attention_____

Bowling	Present Level	I m p r o v e m e n t
Needed		
	Fair – Good – Excellent	Small - Large
Action	_____	_____
Run-up	_____	_____
Rhythm	_____	_____
Control	_____	_____
Variety	_____	_____
Strike-rate	_____	_____
Awareness	_____	

Aspects Needing Attention_____

Wicket-keeping	Present Level	Improvement Needed
	Fair – Good – Excellent	Small - Large
Fast bowling	_____	_____
Slow bowling	_____	_____
Footwork	_____	_____
Glovework	_____	_____
Team motivation	_____	_____
Awareness	_____	

Aspects Needing Attention_____

The Winning Edge

Fielding

	Present Level Fair – Good – Excellent	Improvement Needed Small - Large
Groundwork		
Throwing		
Catching - close to wicket		
- in the deep		
Awareness		

Aspects Needing Attention_____

Tactics and Captaincy

	Present Level Fair – Good – Excellent	Improvement Needed Small - Large
Reading the game		
Observing weaknesses		
Awareness		
Pre-game planning		
One-day games		
Limited overs games		
Three-day games		

Aspects Needing Attention_____

This chart can be printed out from the CD-rom

Wagon Wheels

Wagon wheels are easy, practical, accurate and quick. They help you to pinpoint your areas of strength and weakness. They can be used by individual batsmen and bowlers, and by captains and teams as a whole.

You can even use them to discover the strengths and weaknesses of your opponents.

The precise knowledge they reveal will give you renewed confidence to exploit your strengths. They will also tell you exactly where your weaknesses are, so that you can concentrate your efforts to improve.

Wagon wheels can be highly motivational when setting goals for a match. You know exactly what happened last time – so you can target and measure the improvement this time.

And during the match, the captain can use the wagon wheels from previous matches to help him set fields, either *for* individual bowlers or *against* opposing batsmen. He can also use them to ensure that the best fielders are always in the best positions.

Ask your scorer to keep wagon wheels of your individual and team batting and bowling performances in each match. There is a case for keeping charts for each of the opposition's batsmen and bowlers, too, so that your team can plan how best to play against them next time.

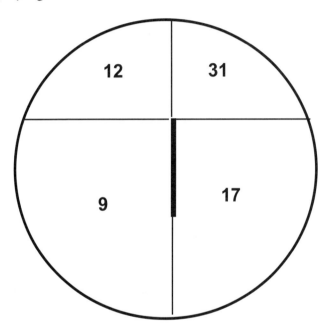

Above is a summary wagon wheel of a bowler who conceded 69 runs in an innings. The chart clearly indicates that he strayed down the leg-side too often and probably bowled too short

Blank wagon wheel charts can be printed out from the CD-rom

Practice Diary

Your brain is designed to forget. Anything you haven't done for three weeks will be fading in your memory. So, at the beginning of each week, before and during the season, keep a diary of your targets, activities and progress. Use the previous charts to identify your priorities for each week, and keep notes of exactly what you plan to do and what you actually did.

	Plan	Actual
Week beginning		
Goals		
1		
2		
3		
4		
Monday		
Tuesday		
Wednesday		
Thursday		
Friday		
Saturday		
Sunday		
Comments for the week		

This chart can be printed out from the CD-rom

Performance Records

After every match, add the details of your performance to your records. Take time to make them as accurate and complete as you can. Make notes about how you felt, how you played, what you learned during the game, what you want to remember about your performance in the future.

After a while these records will increasingly motivate you to do well, and they will prove your progress in hard facts.

My performance today

Batting

Date	
Opponents	
Match (league, cup etc.)	
Wicket conditions	
Batting position	
Runs	
Balls faced	
How scored	
How out	
Type of bowler	
Type of delivery	
Shot attempted	
Where caught	
Comments	

Bowling

Date	
Opponents	
Match (league, cup etc.)	
Wicket conditions	
Overs	
Maidens	
Runs	
Wickets	
Missed chances	
No balls	
Wides	
Bowling spells	
Bowled	
LBW	
Caught	
Caught & bowled	
Stumped	
Comments	

Fielding

Date	
Opponents	
Match (league, cup etc.)	
Wicket conditions	
Catches	
Run Outs	
Misfields	
Runs lost	
Catches dropped	
Stumpings (if WK)	
Comments	

**A more comprehensive version of this chart
is on the CD-rom**

End of Season

At the end of each season work out your personal averages, by type of match and overall. Write down the "do's" and "don'ts" from that season. Try to learn from your experiences, but accentuate the positive aspects, whatever they are.

Then set your targets for runs, wickets and catches for the next season. Write them down and put them in a sealed envelope. Don't look at it again until just before the first game.

Now do something completely different for a while. Forget cricket. But start some fitness work specifically for strength and flexibility well in advance of the next season.

In a nutshell, take a break, and be prepared.

7.

TIPS FOR BUDDING CAPTAINS

(and the rest of the team)

Work harder than the others - be more enthusiastic - set an example all the time.

As captain, you can have a great influence on the relationship between the players as individuals and their performance as a team. There's no satisfaction in playing in a losing team even if you did score a hundred, or take five wickets. Each player needs to accept the responsibility that he's there to do a job. An extra 10 per cent effort and commitment from each player, and everyone trying their utmost throughout the match - that's the difference between winning and losing. That determination and inspiration starts from the captain.

Concentrate on what you control - and what you can control if you try. For instance, ask team members to help each other during a season. Let them pair off to help identify weaknesses, and then work together to overcome them. Bowlers can help batsmen deal with particular deliveries that often get them out, while batsmen can help bowlers contribute more runs at the bottom of the batting order.

Don't worry about anything outside your control, including what the opposition are thinking. But try constantly to improve your ability to "read" and respond to the game and the players. The better you are at these skills, the more likely you are to lead a winning side.

Try to work out, man by man, how you're going to beat the other team. Running in to bowl, keeping a line and length, and hoping for the best is not what's needed. You need to plan, and above all you need to experiment.

If you're up against a stronger side, do things differently from the start. Open your attack with slow bowlers, ask a big hitter to open the innings. Annoy them, disturb their concentration, provoke them into reacting and perhaps making their own mistakes.

Whenever you sense the opposition is getting on top, change the rhythm of the game. If you can't get a wicket, if nothing's happening, make it happen. Try something different, move the field, change the bowling, bowl another line or angle, mix the bowling up, change the field again. Try bowlers who don't bowl regularly. And when you do get on top, make sure you stay there. Keep your grip on the game and finish the job. But never lose sight of your own plan. You thought the batsmen out before the match, now you have to do it on the field.

Seek the opinions of the wicket-keeper (he always has the best view) and the other members of the team. Consulting others is not weakness - especially if you follow one of their suggestions and it works.

Think about targets. What will it take to win this game? Set those targets, make sure everyone knows them and their part in achieving them.

For example, if you're playing a limited overs game and you know that most winning sides score singles at an average rate of 2.5 per over or better, set a target of at least three singles an over, whatever else you score. Twos, threes, boundaries and extras are bonuses, and don't count. Three singles an over will win the game.

Value your wicket. The great players have always put a high value on their wicket. They loathe giving the opposition the satisfaction of dismissing them. And we all know that you can't score runs back in the pavilion. So encourage everyone - tailenders included - to value their wicket. A few extra runs from the tailenders may win the match - so tell them, convince them. Discuss their potential runs contribution before the match, not just when they go out to bat.

In every match, there's at least one chance for a direct hit on the stumps. Sometimes, it will win the game. The team that wants to win has to take that chance. Miss it, and the game may have gone with it. So keep your fielders keen and on their toes.

Praise success - but don't blame the player who makes a mistake. It wasn't deliberate, and he feels worse about it than anybody. So give him support, encouragement. Next time he might win the game for you. Let him see that confidence in your response now.

Will-Power and Commitment

Will-power and commitment can win matches. Underdogs win when they believe they can. Favourites lose when they fear losing. The difference is attitude rather than ability.

Far too many teams don't hate losing enough. They lose too easily, they fold too easily. And they only go for a win when they're sure they can't lose. Yet cricket isn't like that. There is always risk. You have to manage risk, and take it. There's no point in simply trying to avoid it.

At any level - school, grade, league, first-class or test – the truth about winning is as brutal as it is simple. If you want to beat the best, you have to work harder than them, and then some. You also need players who burn with ambition, who will die for each other, who will never give in. That commitment comes best from shared intense experiences at a young age.

Jack Potter tells a story about the Australian U-19 team which he coached at the Australian Cricket Academy in 1990. They were playing the touring England U-19 team, which included John Crawley,

Darren Gough and Dominic Cork, all of whom went on to play test cricket.

At the pre-match meeting, Jack asked the players to remember something special from the previous games. It should be an achievement, he told them, by one of the other members of the team - one which they were proud of, but which they thought nobody else had noticed.

After a few moments, batsman Ken Vowles mentioned an incident during the previous match of the tour. He had approached their quick bowler Stephen Cottrell when the side was wilting in the field in a temperature of 104 degrees F. Vowles wanted to encourage him. England's sixth wicket partnership was already worth 50 on a low, slow wicket, and the match was slipping away.

He said 'Cotts, we're relying on you. If you don't get a wicket this over, we're gone'. In the very next over "Cotts" broke the stand when he clean bowled Noon for 35. The Australians were back in the game. 'We just exchanged winks. I was so proud of him', he said.

After that, the stories came flooding out. Jack confesses that by the end of that session he could not trust himself to speak. The team bonding was so intense he could almost touch it. "I thought I knew that team, and what went on between them. But I had no idea. They were ready to die for each other, and now they all knew it".

Next day, they went onto the field at Perth and beat the cream of England's young cricketers by an innings and two runs, inside two days. Stephen Cottrell took six for 40 in England's first innings of 71, which closed just after lunch on the first day. He took 10 for exactly 100 in the match.

Jack knows, with an unshakeable certainty, exactly what inspired that astonishing performance. Collective will-power and the total and passionate commitment of every player to the team.

That is a goal every team and every member of it should always be striving to achieve. However difficult or distant it might seem, it is always worth the effort. "One for all, and all for one" - that's the key, especially when your team's in trouble.

The results can be awesome.

8.

FITNESS AND TRANSFERRING SKILLS

The fit cricketer can play harder for longer, recover quicker, concentrate better and perform more effectively. He will be more successful.

So, like all sportsmen, cricketers need to get fit, keep themselves fit, and be fit for each game. That means plenty of foundation work, ideally with a strong aerobic base. The emphasis should be on building up strength, flexibility, speed and power. If you don't have any knowledge or experience of fitness programmes and aerobics go to your local gym or sports and leisure centre. Ask them to set up a special programme for you. And there are plenty of good practical books on these subjects to help you along.

Many cricketers, especially those still at school or college, play other sports in the "off season", and some of these can be turned to advantage in preparing for the following cricket season.

Any activity which assists fitness, speed of movement and sharpens reflexes is useful to a cricketer. Sports such as squash, badminton, baseball, athletics, basketball, softball, table-tennis, soccer and hockey are all recommended.

Some other sports, where injury is likely, should be avoided. Rugby, Australian rules football, even skiing, can all be hazardous to the cricketer. Even a non-contact sport like golf, which so many cricketers love and play well, can be a risk. If you are a bowler, a round of golf will not do your back any favours. The back-twisting movements can be particularly aggravating.

Meanwhile, your goal should be to start the next season as match fit as possible. Your fitness programme should gradually build up to that moment, and many coaches encourage a four-phase timetable.

Immediately after the end of the last season allow yourself to relax and recover. Just maintain some gentle activities, anything you enjoy and which keeps the body toned up. Work on the recovery from past injuries if necessary.

During mid-winter, gradually start stepping up your fitness programme, concentrating on speed drills and flexibility.

Then, as the new season approaches, step up again. Keep the flexibility and speed part of your programme going, but move the emphasis to building up your strength and power.

Finally, get back in the nets and concentrate on your cricket skills. And at the same time taper off the fitness programme to a level which will maintain your standard of fitness throughout the season. This means focussing on speed and acceleration, agility and turning speed, and general body flexibility.

Improving Your Reactions

Two of the most important qualities in any player of ball games are hand/eye co-ordination and speed of reflex. For the cricketer, they are crucial.

Since every player – even regular members of the No 11 club - bats from time to time, we can all be faced with situations which demand a decision and action within less than half a second. That's quick.

The eye leads – the body follows. At least, that's the plan. A sequence of several processes is involved. There is no time for conscious thought, but this is what should happen within that half a second:

a. See and register the ball

b. Decide on the shot

c. Initiate the movement of the feet and hands

d. Complete the movement, with the maximum force of the shot coinciding exactly with the moment the bat hits the ball.

If you got it right, you will have "timed" the shot to perfection, and sent the ball exactly where you wanted at maximum speed.

Here are two simple techniques to develop your eye/hand co-ordination.

1. When practising fielding, ask someone to stand at a slight angle from the line of the ball coming towards you. As usual, you run to field each ball. But just before you reach it, they hold up a card with a number or letter on it. You have to read that number or letter, and shout it out as you throw the ball in to the wicket-keeper.

2. Write out a card of capital letters, ten letters in a row, and ten rows down. Any letters in any order. You now have a solid block of 100 random letters. Set them up at eye-level, just far enough away from you to be readable.

Now – as fast as you can – read out loud the first letter of the first line, then the last letter of the first line. Now read the second letter of the first line followed by the ninth. Now the third followed by the eighth. And so on. Complete line one, then drop down to line two, and so on down to the last line.

Next, try reading in reverse order. Try reading while standing on one leg. Try while juggling with one, two or three balls. Each time, the objective is speed and accuracy.

Make a new chart once you start remembering the sequences of letters.

Use these techniques regularly and you will improve your reaction times and your co-ordination. You will also find that you don't get distracted so easily when playing in a match.

Diet

Avoid fatty foods. Eat regularly. Keep your diet simple and good.

Try to build up your strength for a match tomorrow by eating a good balanced meal the evening before. Steak and vegetables are infinitely better for you than a hamburger and chips.

Take a light breakfast, and during the match only eat carbohydrate foods - rice, pasta, potatoes and the like, with a little sauce or light addition if you must to make them more palatable. At this time of the day avoid heavy, protein-laden or fatty foods.

At tea, or later in the day, take foods that release energy quickly, such as fruit, jam sandwiches or cake. Glucose tablets, or even a few sweets, will give you instant energy. Or you could add sugar to your drink.

Try to drink squashes or water during the match. They are more efficient than tea or coffee in helping you to recover from de-hydration.

After the match, drink squash first, and then have a meal. If you want a beer have it later in the evening.

9.

SPORTSMANSHIP

The very word "cricket" is often used all over the world to mean sportsmanship and fair play. Even today, "it isn't cricket" is still a quick way of describing something that is basically unfair.

Cricket has always been a tough and competitive game - sometimes fiercely competitive - but we should always value and observe the best traditions of the game.

That means playing hard but fair - competing but not cheating - recognising and accepting your opponents' successes, while trying to be even more successful yourself - being generous in victory and magnanimous in defeat.

In other words, go into each game with respect for the game itself. And try to leave each game with the finest traditions for sportsmanship at least unspoiled, and at best enhanced.

10.

WHAT HAPPENS NEXT

Now that you have read this little manual once, you know what it takes to be successful on the cricket field. But knowing is only the start. What matters most of all is turning that knowledge into action.

You may also be tempted to think that your new knowledge will somehow automatically improve your game. It won't. It will happen when you make it happen.

Now's the time to look at the CD, and set up the charts and records on your computer.

Then, read through this book again. Re-read the sections in this book that deal with your specific problems and disappointments today. Turn to this book again and again in the future, immediately and whenever you have difficulties.

No matter what your current standard or future aspirations, the secrets and techniques that we've explained will help make a real difference to your performance, your progress and your enjoyment of this extraordinary game.

And remember - you will have gained all the benefits this book can offer only when you can read it through and truthfully say that all of its ideas are now an everyday part of your cricketing life.

Until that day dawns, we suggest that you keep it with you, and dip into it regularly.

And good luck

APPENDIX

WINNING EDGE CHECK-LIST FOR COACHES

The following is not intended to be a comprehensive check-list for coaches. It is intended to act as a reminder of some of the often forgotten aspects of coaching.

Players' Personal Ambitions
- What do I want to achieve?
- How am I going to get there?
- What's the first step on that road?
- then, what's the next step, and the next...

Personal Performances - and Improvements
- the elements involved in maximising personal potential
- mental training
- physical training
- confidence building
- goal-oriented progress
- isolating and solving performance problems

Captaincy
- reading the game and the players
- getting the best out of your team
- ask questions of them
- ask for performance from them
- assign tasks
- stretch them mentally
- support and encourage
- tactics on and off the field

Reviewing Strengths and Weaknesses
- what do we know about the other team
- what do they know about us

Your Role in a Team Game
- as an individual
- as part of the team

Batting
- batting tactics and targets
- reading each bowler's delivery
- selecting the right shot
- playing with confidence

Bowling
- attacking the batsman
- developing a bowling strategy against each batsman

Fielding
- attacking the ball on the ground
- fast returns, close to wicket and from the deep
- how to throw fast and accurately